Fire in My Heart

Learning to Preach the Word of God

by Jarrod Jacobs

ONE STONE
BIBLICAL RESOURCES

Published by:
One Stone Press
979 Lovers Lane
Bowling Green, KY 42103

Printed in the United States of America

ISBN-10: 1-941422-16-0
ISBN-13: 978-1-941422-16-8

ONE STONE
BIBLICAL RESOURCES

www.onestone.com

Introduction

Through the years, folks have asked me when I knew I wanted to become a preacher of the gospel. This was hard for me to answer, because it seemed like I always knew I wanted to be a preacher. The "how" had not been thought out, but I knew I wanted to preach the gospel in some capacity. On the last Sunday in December 1991, everything changed when I preached my first sermon in Oblong, Illinois. I was still in high school at this time and was a member of the Ellettsville church of Christ in Ellettsville, Indiana. In 1992, I attended a preacher training program with brother Johnie Edwards who was preaching there at the time. Johnie began a year-long study with me and a few others who have since gone on to become preachers and leaders in the churches they attend. These classes were three hours long every week with homework due at the following week's study. It was an intense year for sure, but it was very rewarding. Brother Johnie is known for his preacher training programs, but I hold our class as special because it was the "guinea pig" class from whence came all the others!

Since then, I have had opportunities to instruct other young preachers. Then, in 2014, the student became the teacher when I began a preacher training program in Caneyville, Kentucky.

This volume contains the material my students study for the first three months of training. The material in this book is a combination of the material once studied with Johnie, along with my own study and experiences. In addition to studying this material, students plan expository studies, topical studies, and other such "homework" to help prepare for the real world as a preacher of the gospel.

Whatever I do as a preacher, and whatever I might teach future preachers, is a result of the study Johnie did with me in the early 1990's. Therefore, this volume is dedicated to Johnie Edwards, a man who helped me in those early years to reach my goal of becoming a preacher of the gospel.

Contents

~ 1 ~
General Observations on Preaching

Introduction

I.   Preaching is almost as old as man himself. The first preaching was done by God to the first people, Adam and Eve. He told them what He expected in His garden, and the consequences for disobedience (Genesis 2:15-17).

II. The word "preach" (and all its variations: -ing, -ed, -er) is found 91 times in the Bible. God emphasizes this for a reason! Specifically, we see that any time folks learn the truth of salvation, God chooses that the message be delivered man-to-man.

   A. Noah was called a preacher by God (2 Peter 2:5).

   B. Jonah was sent by God to go and preach to the people of Nineveh (Jonah 1:2, 3:2; Matthew 12:41).

   C. All of the Old and New Testament prophets were "mouths" for God. Example: Ezekiel (3:17, 6:11) and Jeremiah (6:16-17).

III. When someone wishes to preach the gospel of God, this person is taking on a responsibility that is not to be taken lightly. One's preaching affects his own soul as well as the souls of all others he comes in contact with in his life!

Discussion

I. God has always used preaching as a means of instruction and warning.

   A. God used John the Baptist in this work (Matthew 3:1; Luke 3:3).

   B. Jesus was a preacher as well (Matthew 4:17, 23).

   C. The apostles were preachers of God's word in the Limited Commission and Great Commision (Matthew 10:1-7; Mark 16:15-16; Acts 20:7-9, 15:35).

   D. The early Christians spread the gospel wherever they could (Acts 8:4, 11:19-21).

   E. Read and study 1 Corinthians 1:18-21 to see the necessity of preaching the cross. This is the reason for preaching!

   F. Our work is accepting the responsibility to teach others what we have been taught (2 Timothy 2:2; Hebrews 5:12-14; 1 Timothy 4:16; 2 Timothy 4:1-5).

   G. Assignment #1: Memorize the verses listed above.

II. Don't preach if you can keep from it.

   A. This may seem counterintuitive, but it is true. A man has to be truly dedicated if he is going to preach the gospel. If you think there is something else you would rather do than preach, then please do it!

      1. Anything less than full commitment to this work will be seen by those listening to you preach.

      2. Anything less than full commitment to this work will be evident in how you study, how you work and your interest in studying with others, as well as how you treat others.

3. Giving less than 100% may work in many secular jobs, but never in preaching!

B. Read James 3:1.

C. Remember that a preacher is a steward of God's word (1 Corinthians 4:1-2). This means a preacher is accountable for what he does, what he does not do and how he uses his time.

D. Matthew 12:36-37 teaches that words affect one's salvation! It is that serious!

III. Some traits preachers need to observe

A. Often it is the small things that can make a difference, just as much as the big things. There are some traits that ought to be in preachers. Some of them are found in Scripture, and some of them are indicative of good common sense.

B. Below are some of the traits that a preacher ought to have.

1. Be enthusiastic.

   a. Ezekiel 6:11

   b. Titus 2:14

   c. Acts 8:30

2. Be friendly.

   a. This is a must! It is imperative to be friendly with all people. Do NOT show favoritism.

   b. Proverbs 18:24

   c. When you are new in a congregation, people are patient and give you time to adjust, but make sure to learn folks' names soon—and use them!

3. Dress neatly.

    a. Dress reflects our attitude and our thoughts about work.

    b. Watch your body odor!

    c. A blue blazer goes with many things.

4. Be mannerly.

    a. Good manners in a hospital or home are key.

    b. When in a home for a meal, make sure to eat and show your gratitude.

    c. Write thank you cards when invited into a home, in a gospel meeting, etc.

    d. For many, the sermons you preach will not be heard as loudly as your actions in how you treat others.

5. Always be punctual.

6. Be tactful.

7. Be organized.

8. Be an optimistic person.

    a. Optimism is key to having a good work.

    b. Some preachers become bitter, and this is a recipe for disaster in their work. It is also something that jeopardizes one's soul (James 3:14; Ephesians 4:31; Hebrews 12:15).

9. Remember, you are in a work that puts you in contact with people on a daily basis. Therefore, learn how to get along with people.

10. Accept constructive criticism.

a. Everyone is capable of error, whether it is sinful (Romans 3:23) or something not being done very well.

b. Sometimes your wife, or a concerned Christian, cares and wants to help make you better in your work.

c. Therefore, a preacher needs the ability to take criticism!

11. Be humble! Don't be a know it all (1 Peter 5:5-6).

12. Make time for study (2 Timothy 2:15; Revelation 1:3).

13. Make sure to pay your bills! To not do so is dishonest and theft!

14. Can you think of other qualities a preacher needs?

_____

_____

_____

_____

Conclusion

I. Assignment #2: Write an article (100 words or less) about "What Makes a Good Preacher."

II. Assignment #3: Read 1 and 2 Timothy and Titus every week in our preacher training program. These books are the words of an older preacher to two younger preachers, showing them how to preach. In like manner, these books teach preachers today how to preach!

~ 2 ~
Sermon Preparation

Introduction

I.   In this lesson, focus is upon sermon preparation, outlining sermons, and the like.

II. One responsibility every preacher has is sermon preparation. Public speaking is one way you'll be spreading the gospel.

 A. A sermon is a presentation of religious or spiritual material in a public manner.

 B. If I learn to organize my thoughts and speak effectively in public, it helps me speak to folks in private as well.

 C. 2 Timothy 4:1-5

III. Every preacher needs to realize the importance of his task. Why?

 A. Souls are at stake (Matthew 16:26).

 B. Judgment is awaiting the preacher of the gospel (James 3:1).

Discussion

I.   Some things to keep in mind when preparing sermons

 A. The purpose of the sermon

  1. Preach to change the hearts of men.

      a. Matthew 18:3

      b. Acts 3:19

  2. To save self and others

      a. 1 Timothy 4:16

      b. A two-fold purpose

B. Plan the introduction and conclusion carefully in every sermon. The introduction explains the purpose for speaking, and the conclusion reminds folks of what was said.

C. KEY: Do not have a "friend" in the assembly! (The point being that a preacher cannot be swayed to change the message of the gospel in fear or favor of who is in the assembly.)

D. Your life must be in harmony with the sermon.

  1. Romans 2:21-22

  2. Ezra 7:10

  3. Acts 1:1

E. Organization is a necessity in every sermon. Good organization helps maintain the topic.

  1. Books that help in the preparation of sermons:

      a. Preaching books written by Tom Holland

      b. *The Seven Laws Of Teaching* by Gregory

      c. *Preaching That Changes Lives* by Michael Fabarez

      d. *How To Preach Without Notes* by Koller

  2. These are a few examples of sermon books that are helpful, but remember—these books are written by men, subject to error and a man's opinion about

matters. They are helpful, but the Bible is the best book to show you how to preach sermons.

    a. Examples of Jesus' preaching (parables as well as His teaching in the temple, example: John 7-8)

    b. Examples of Peter's preaching (Acts 2, 10, etc.)

    c. Examples of Paul's preaching (Acts 13, 17, etc.)

F. Always know more about the subject than you intend to present.

    1. "Preach from the overflow." Therefore, make sure and be full of the word (Ezekiel 3:1-3).

    2. Sermons should be a portion of a much greater and deeper study.

    3. It is like drinking water from a reservoir—in so doing, you can preach for years and never run dry.

II. The preacher as a watchman

A. Ezekiel 3:17-19

B. The watchman has 2 duties:

    1. Hear God's word.

    2. Warn the people.

C. Both the preacher and the people have a responsibility in the sermon (preaching/hearing).

D. The apostle Paul is a great example of this (Acts 20:17-27).

III. The need for balance

A. A preacher's sermons should have balance. This balance is determined by God (2 Timothy 4:1-5).

B. It is good to keep a list of sermons to see what sermons have been preached, what subjects, etc.

C. Acts 20:27: Are you preaching "all the counsel of God?"

IV. Finding sermon ideas

    A. Sometimes, preachers say they cannot find sermon ideas. There is access to the greatest "sermon book" ever: the Bible!

    B. Other sources are sermon outline books written by men who want to help preachers:

      1. *Sermon Outlines* by Hinton

      2. *Franklin Road Sermons*

      3. *Book, Chapter, and Verse* by Floyd Thompson

      4. *Preach the Word* edited by Earl Robertson

      5. *Brewer's Sermons* by G.C. Brewer

      6. *Sermon Outlines on First Principles* by C.C. Crawford

      7. *Porter Sermon Outlines* by Curtis Porter

      8. *Sermons Inside and Out* by Hoyt Houchen

      9. *The Gospel Preacher Vol. 1 & 2* by Benjamin Franklin

      10. *Sermons, Chapel Talks, and Debates* by A.G. Freed

      11. *"Sermons By Pickup"* by Harry Pickup, Sr.

      12. *The Gospel Plan of Salvation* by T.W. Brents

      13. *Sermon Outlines* edited by Mike Willis

      14. *Gospel Meeting Sermons* by Johnie Edwards

      15. *First Century Preaching* edited by Jimmy Tuten

      16. *Gospel Sermons at the Mosque* by Harris J. Dark

      17. *God Hath Spoken* by Harris J. Dark

      18. *Preaching That Changes Lives* by Irven Lee

   C. Study a chapter, a verse, a word or words in the Bible.

   D. Keep a pen and paper close. Sermon ideas are found in many places.

      1. Sometimes, an idea for a sermon comes to you only once, so write it down when you get it!

      2. Keep a "sermon idea" folder.

V.   How preachers need to preach

   A. "Speak forth the words of truth and soberness" (Acts 26:25).

   B. Speak with an "open mouth" (Matthew 5:2; Acts 8:35, 10:35).

   C. Speak boldly (Acts 9:27-28, 13:46, 14:3, 19:8, 26:26; Ephesians 6:19-20).

   D. Speak in love (Ephesians 4:15).

   E. Speak so as to please God and not man (Galatians 1:10; 1 Thessalonians 2:1-5).

VI. Some lessons to be learned about preaching through Paul's example

   A. Consistency (1 Corinthians 4:17)

   B. Not ashamed of the gospel (Romans 1:16-17)

   C. Preaching the whole counsel of God (Acts 20:27)

   D. Believed what he was saying (Acts 27:25; 2 Timothy 1:12; 1 Corinthians 4:13)

   E. The attitude while preaching (1 Thessalonians 2:1-12)

VII. Real needs in today's pulpit

   A. Nehemiah 8:1-8

      1. An open book

2. Preaching which brings people to respect God's word and repent

3. Understandable preaching: We are in a "communication business!" If we fail to communicate effectively, we are wasting our time and the time of those who listen.

4. Preaching that demands personal applications: There is hesitation or neglect in this area at times.

B. Sermons that cause men to tremble (Acts 24:25)

C. Sermons with life in them (Ezekiel 6:11)

D. Uncompromising sermons (Exodus 10:24-25; Galatians 2:4-5)

E. Sermons that:

1. Cut/prick the heart (Acts 7:54, 2:37)

2. Turn the world upside down (Acts 17:6)

3. Convict in such a way that the world knows a prophet has been among them (Ezekiel 2:5)

F. God has spoken and we need to listen (Hebrews 1:1-2).

VIII. Outlining a sermon

A. Now that you have learned about sermons and learned to appreciate what a sermon is to do in the lives of people, below is a simple form of sermon outlining.

B. Sermons can be outlined properly and, as a result, be used over and over again as the need arises. (If you already outline like our example below, great. If not, please give this pattern a try.)

C. Example of a sermon outline:

Title of Sermon

Introduction

I.

    A.

    B.

II.

    A.

    B.

Discussion

I.   Main thought

    A. Sub-thought

    B.

        1. Further thought connected with the above sub-thought

        2.

            a.

            b.

II.

III.

(Etc.)

Conclusion

I.   A short summary of the sermon

II.   Every sermon must contain the plan of salvation for the alien sinner as well as the erring child of God.

~ 3 ~
Funeral Sermons

Introduction

I. In this study, the focus is on a different type of sermon that preachers are called upon to preach—specifically, the funeral sermon.

II. While this is not a duty that one must do in order to be considered faithful by God or something one does in order to get to Heaven, preaching a funeral sermon is a privilege and an honor, and it allows an opportunity to teach the gospel to people that might not otherwise have an opportunity to hear.

Discussion

I. The funeral

    A. Funerals are the occasion when a family stops and reflects upon the life of a deceased loved one.

    B. Of course, friends, loved ones, neighbors, etc., may attend and pay respects to the family who is enduring the loss.

    C. What part does a preacher have in such occasions?

        1. Be someone who gives comfort to the family (see Romans 12:15).

        2. Be someone who shows some guidance and leadership in a time when the family is emotionally distraught—

for example, determining the order of funeral services, helping to get singers, finding a song leader for congregational singing, etc. If it is a member of the church, the preacher may make sure the congregation knows about the death, etc.

3. Be present to pray with the family (before, during and after the funeral), whether it is offering prayers in the home, at the funeral home, etc.

II. Thoughts about the preacher's work when funerals occur

A. When called upon to preach a funeral

1. Go to the home of the family in the day(s) before the funeral to talk and especially to pray. This is not to be an all-day visit but to stop in and let them know you genuinely care.

2. If possible, go to the funeral home when the family goes. The first "look" at this time can be one of the hardest times.

3. If the viewing/visitation is one day and the funeral the next, make sure to attend the viewing.

   a. Again, it is not necessary to make it an all-night visit, but your presence for a while at the funeral home can make a world of difference with people.

4. On the day of the funeral

   a. Be there a minimum of 30 minutes early. This allows time to arrive at the funeral home at a reasonable time and not be rushed.

   b. Your presence eases folks' concern in knowing you are responsible for your duty.

      c. By being there, it gives you the opportunity to speak with some people and still maintain time to collect your thoughts before the service time.

      d. Always be early rather than on time.

  B. During the visitation and funeral times

      1. Be watchful for folks who might be good prospects for the gospel.

      2. At times, such occasions as this will get folks thinking about their souls and if they are right with God (Ecclesiastes 7:1-2).

  C. The reason for preaching the gospel at funerals is this: What is said at a funeral does not send the dead person to Heaven or Hell. However, what is said at a funeral may send those listening to Heaven or Hell.

  D. A funeral is not a time to tell jokes or reminisce and close with prayer. Sadly, more and more people are wanting funerals to be like this.

  E. Funerals are a time for the living to consider their lives and make changes. Use every opportunity to preach the gospel to an assembled crowd.

III. Types of funeral sermons

  A. Recognize that death comes to those of every age (Ecclesiastes 9:5; Hebrews 9:27).

  B. Job observes that "kings, counselors of the earth, princes, (the rich), wicked, prisoners, small and great, slave, and free, infants" have all seen death (Job 3:13-19).

  C. Death is the great equalizer! It is said that in death and in Christ are the only two places where all men are equal.

D. Thus, preachers need to be prepared to perform funerals for folks of all ages and stages of life. Also, preachers need to be prepared to preach funerals for Christians and non-Christians.

E. Assignment #1: Prepare funeral sermons for the following:

   1. A small baby

   2. A teenage girl

   3. A teenage boy

   4. An old man (Christian)

   5. An old woman (Christian)

   6. A man in general

   7. A woman in general

Conclusion

I. For more thoughts concerning funeral sermons and how they ought to be done, please read Addendum 2.

II. Assignment #2: Make a new folder entitled "Funeral Sermons." Keep some sermons there as well as ideas specifically for funeral sermons. Sometimes there is very little notice for preaching a funeral sermon.

III. Assignment #3: Write an article (100 words) on "The Preacher and the Funeral."

~ 4 ~
Wedding Sermons

Introduction

I.   Another type of sermon a preacher needs to prepare is the wedding sermon.

II. Assignment #1: Make a "Wedding Sermons" folder for sermons, as well as ideas, sayings and good thoughts that are useful when performing a wedding ceremony.

III. This is not a duty that one must do in order to be considered faithful by God or something one does in order to get to Heaven, but preaching a wedding sermon allows the gospel to be preached to people that might not otherwise have an opportunity to hear God's word.

Discussion

I.   The wedding

    A. Weddings are occasions of joy at the union of a man and woman in matrimony for life.

    B. Jesus attended a wedding while upon this earth (John 2:1-11).

        1. This was the occasion for Christ's first miracle.

    C. Weddings are a special day in the lives of two people. This day begins their life as husband and wife. Please note there is a difference between a wedding and a marriage!

    1. Do you know the difference?

    2. What is the difference between a wedding and a marriage?

  D. The first marriage in history is the marriage of
_____ (Genesis 2:18-25).

    1. In this text, we see:

      a. The three involved in marriage: God, man and woman

      b. The plan for marriage: a man and a woman leave their parents to live as their own family.

      c. The intimacy enjoyed in this relationship

    2. Jesus spoke about the permanency of marriage in Matthew 19:4-6. He added, "What therefore God hath joined together, let not man put asunder/ separate."

  E. Folks need to be reminded of the truth in Hebrews 13:4.

  F. Ephesians 5:22-33 has much to say about husbands and wives as Paul uses this relationship to describe Christ and the church.

II. Who can get married?

  A. There are three categories of people who can marry:

    1. Those who have never been married before (Genesis 2:18-24; Matthew 19:4-6).

    2. Widowed people (Romans 7:1-3).

    3. Those who have divorced their spouse for the cause of fornication (Matthew 5:32; 19:9).

  B. The instructions of the Lord are simple and plain. Respect what the Lord has said.

C. Unfortunately, there will come a time when a couple will want to "get married" (i.e., perform the ceremony) but does not have the Scriptural right to be married.

D. What then? What will you do?

III. Other aspects of weddings that demand attention

A. Legal forms

1. In order to legally marry a couple, a marriage license needs to be completed. It is the responsibility of the couple to obtain it, but the preacher completes it.

2. In some states, there may be a need to be bonded, considered "ordained," etc. Each state is different.

a. Indiana, Kentucky and Tennessee require that you be considered a minister of a state-recognized church (i.e., not a cult or a made-up group of some sort, looking for a tax write-off).

b. Make sure to double-check as laws tend to change through the years.

3. Personal practice concerning marriage licenses:

a. Make sure the couple gets it and brings it to the rehearsal.

b. Complete it with the couple and the witnesses.

c. Once the license is complete, give it to one of the mothers to mail. (It will get done!)

B. For a couple wishing to get married in a church building, some questions may arise.

1. "We'd like to bring an organ/keyboard in for the wedding."

    2. "Could we have instrumental music on CD or an mp3 player?"

    3. How do you answer these questions?

Conclusion

I.   Assignment #2: Prepare a sermon for a wedding.

II.   Assignment #3: Write an article (100 words) on "The Preacher and the Wedding."

~ 5 ~
Radio and TV Preaching

Introduction

I.   Evangelism is accomplished in many ways. There is not just one way to spread the gospel.

II.   Be alert for ways to Scripturally spread the gospel.

III. As technology changes, and various advancements come to society, there will be more ways to spread the gospel than previous generations could imagine.

IV.   However, nothing replaces the method of talking to people one-on-one.

V.   As our culture spreads, consider the following ways to deliver God's truth.

Discussion

I.   Radio programs

    A. Live radio preaching is very exciting! This is true with a sermon or radio "call in" program.

        1. Is there Bible authority for doing radio programs? What passage(s) is given to support that radio programs are authorized by God even though radios did not exist in the first century? (This will be questioned.)

———————————————

———————————————

———————————————

———————————————

   2. Radio programs may be a recorded message, so give it a live "feel" and do the program in one take.

B. Radio programs are a great advantage in evangelism. Give some reasons why radio programs are advantageous to spreading the gospel.

———————————————

———————————————

———————————————

———————————————

C. Radio preaching results:

   1. Many conversions have happened because someone heard the gospel over the radio.

   2. There will be preaching in homes and businesses with folks listening to the gospel.

D. "How can I go about making a radio sermon?"

   1. One suggestion: Take a current sermon preached and adapt it to the format of a radio program.

   2. Always be prepared to preach a sermon on the radio. Sometimes, when you're holding a gospel meeting, the brethren may ask you to preach on their radio program.

E. Assignment #1: Make a folder titled "Radio Sermons" to keep sermons made into radio sermons. This folder can hold ideas for new radio sermons as well.

II. Television preaching

   A. While this is not as common as radio preaching, television preaching is becoming more widespread with cable access channels, YouTube, and the like.

   B. There are several similarities between radio and television preaching, but they are not the same!

   C. Do we have Bible authority for doing television programs? What passage(s) is given to support television programs are authorized by God even though televisions did not exist in the first century? (This will be questioned.)

_____

_____

_____

_____

   D. Just as radio programs are a great advantage in evangelism, so are television programs. Give some reasons why television programs are advantageous to spreading the gospel?

_____

_____

_____

_____

   E. As with radio programs, I have held meetings where the brethren had a television program, and they asked me to appear on it. It would be wise to have some extra sermons ready when in a meeting, just in case. (Usually, this will be told to you before you begin the gospel meeting.)

F. Assignment #2: Make a folder titled "Television Sermons" and use it to store those sermons made into television sermons, as well as ideas for sermons to use on television.

III. The internet

A. This includes blogs, Twitter, Facebook, websites, YouTube, etc.

B. This is another way in which preachers of the gospel can "go into all the world!"

C. Like all other forms of teaching, one must make sure that what he writes and posts is true to the Book! (2 Timothy 4:2).

D. Here are some ways folks use the internet to spread the gospel:

1. Daily or weekly blog articles

2. Uploading sermons, bulletins, etc.

3. Use these sites to generate contacts and carry on conversations with folks as you study God's word together.

E. What do you see as a way of spreading the gospel using the technology we have today?

_____

_____

_____

Conclusion

I. Assignment #3: Take the sermons you currently have and prepare them to be used on a 30-minute radio program.

A. Assignment #3a: To help prepare for this work, listen to a radio program.

B. In the beginning, do some programs with someone who currently does radio sermons and work to make that material fit in the allotted time.

II. Assignment #4: Take the sermons and be ready to use them in a television format.

A. Assignment #4a: Watch our television programs. Visit http://www.youtube.com/TheOldPaths1994

~ 6 ~
Types of Sermons

Introduction

I.   Evangelism is accomplished in many ways. There is not just one way to spread the gospel.

II.   As an evangelist, be on the lookout for ways to Scripturally spread the gospel.

III. Preaching sermons is the primary way that you teach others and get God's message to them.

    A. There are different types of sermons a preacher can use as he strives to spread God's message to others.

    B. Know these types of sermons and develop them to present God's word in different ways.

IV.   Remember: preaching is a communication business! Therefore, find ways to effectively communicate the message when preaching.

V.   Some pointers:

    A. Don't Don't repeat repeat yourself yourself! Some preachers are guilty of repeating things over and over again in their sermons.

        1. Sometimes, this is due to a lack of preparation or organization in the sermon.

2. Sometimes it is perceived the job or lesson wasn't done right the first time.

3. Be organized in thoughts, speech and outline.

B. Appropriate transitional phrases are helpful in a sermon.

1. For a good example of transitional phrases, watch the news and notice how a sportscaster uses transitional phrases as he announces the competing teams along with the winning and losing scores.

2. Examples of transitional phrases: "The wise man said," "The Holy Spirit wrote," "Matthew tells us," "The Lord said," etc.

3. Assignment #1: Make a list of 50 transitional phrases that would be helpful in your sermons as you transition between points.

C. Good speech is a good man speaking well!

VI. What are the various types of sermons that a preacher can use?

Discussion

I. Defining our terms

A. To best know what God had in mind when He used terms like "preach," "preaching," "preacher," etc., let us define these terms. (Hint: This is always a good place to start when teaching others.)

B. Sermon—stab or thrust; indicative of the purpose of a religious discourse. "To cut to the heart," as spoken in Acts 2:37.

C. Preach—five Greek words are used, often translated as "preach," "preaching," "preacher," etc.: *kerysso, didasko*, and *–angello*.

1. *Kerysso*—proclaim as a herald. The idea is of one standing in the city square and telling folks the message of their king. Upon letting folks know the message, they understand that they cannot remain passive! Being a herald demands speaking with authority (1 Timothy 4:11; Titus 2:15).

2. *Didasko*—to teach. This is the term used by Jesus in Matthew 28:20.

3. *–angello*—There are three words used in Scripture that have their root as "angello" or "angel." They are: *evangelizo*, *katangello*, and *anangello*.

D. Some people mistakenly make a distinction between teaching and preaching, saying things like, "Evangelists preach to lost people, not to saved people." Or, "You can't 'evangelize' Christians." Men have made this distinction, but it is not found within Scripture. These terms are used interchangeably in the spreading of the gospel, whether to the saved or the unsaved!

E. Therefore, get busy spreading the gospel: heralding, teaching and preaching!

II. Finding sermons

A. Sermon ideas are everywhere. (How are you doing in filling your "Sermon Ideas" folder?)

B. #1 source: the Bible! Continue to read and study, gaining more sermons.

1. Many people (Samuel, Moses, Jesus, Paul, Peter, etc.) have sermons recorded in the Bible. Use them!

2. Assignment #2: Outline the sermon preached by Peter in Acts 2:22-41. Be ready to preach.

C. Places and situations can spark ideas for sermons. Examples: TV ads, newspapers, magazines, tracts, billboards, etc.

D. Every time you hear a preacher preach, come away with at least one sermon. A good preacher will spark your thoughts and give you even more ideas. Hint: If you've paid attention, you'll have acquired at least one sermon from simply studying the lesson this week (hopefully more!).

III. Expository sermons

A. An expository sermon is a sermon that "exposes" what is being taught in a certain text. It could be a verse, a paragraph, a chapter, etc.

B. In these types of sermons, stay focused on the text and get all points from the selected text. Here is an example of an expository sermon: "The Righteous Judgment of God" (Romans 2:1-16).

1. It is "according to truth" (v. 2).

2. No one will escape (v. 3).

3. It is just and fair (v. 6, 11).

4. Two groups of people will be judged (v. 7-10).

5. It will happen on a definite "day" (v. 16).

6. The standard of judgment will be the gospel (v. 16).

7. Why has God waited this long to judge the world? (v. 4).

8. Conclusion: Are you ready for the judgment day?

C. Assignment #3: Write an expository sermon based on Psalm 23, taking a point from each verse.

IV. Topical sermons

    A. Topical sermons focus on a certain topic or theme. Instead of finding one text and preaching it, search the Bible for verses related to a certain topic.

    B. With this study, the preacher presents what the Bible (both Old and New Testaments) says about the topic.

    C. How to do this:

        1. When studying a particular topic, find every verse where the Bible mentions that subject, then read and study those passages in their context.

        2. Examples: baptism, instrumental music/singing, love, grace, the church, worship, etc.

    D. Topical sermons can include acrostic sermons, where one chooses a subject and uses each letter of the subject as a point in the sermon. For examples of these, please read Addendum 3, where several examples of acrostic sermons are listed.

    E. Have you made a topical sermon yet? If so, what is the topic of the sermon?

    F. Assignment #4: How are you doing on your Bible reading of 1 and 2 Timothy and Titus? Take the book of 1 Timothy and write down sermon topics seen in that book. Then do the same thing for 2 Timothy and Titus. Add findings to the "Sermon Ideas" folder.

V. Biographical sermons

    A. These sermons focus upon the life of a certain person, examine what they did, and lessons to be learned from their lives (Romans 15:4; 1 Corinthians 10:11).

B. This type of preaching demands a good knowledge of the person, life during the time they lived, and the challenges that person faced in order to make applications to the present day.

C. Since God is no respecter of persons, there is access to the biographies of people whose lives are worthy of following and those whose decisions ought to be avoided.

D. Assignment #5: Name some Bible characters (their examples could be good or evil) whose lives would make good biographical sermons. Add this list to your "Sermon Ideas" folder.

VI. Textual sermons

A. Textual sermons are related to expository sermons in that they both begin with a text of Scripture, an analysis of it, etc. The difference is that a textual sermon uses that verse as a jumping off point for the rest of the sermon.

B. As with the above, respect the context of the verses when preaching textual sermons.

C. Example of a textual sermon: preaching on Hebrews 13:8 and then speaking about how Christ is the same yesterday, today, and forever in His doctrine, etc.

D. Example of a textual sermon: preaching on Luke 15:11-32 and focusing your attention in the sermon on the father of the prodigal son.

Conclusion

I. The list above is not intended to be exhaustive, but these are some of the major categories into which sermons will fall.

II. Regardless of the type of sermon chosen to convey the gospel message, remember, the marching orders are made clear in 2 Timothy 4:2. Never deviate from these orders!

III. Regardless of the type of sermon, make sure and "bring it home" to those listening. Make applications to their lives, so they can see how the Bible applies to all of us in the 21st century. Make sure folks are cut to the heart when you're preaching (Acts 2:37).

~ 7 ~
Building a Library

Introduction

I.   A valuable part of a preacher's study is the use of good books, commentaries, Bible dictionaries, and the like. Books are tools a preacher uses, just as a hammer and saw are tools to the carpenter.

II. Such books are helpful to a preacher's study of various Bible subjects. Some books give insight into the lives of the people from Old and New Testaments, causing an appreciation of the people.

III. Ecclesiastes 12:12: "Of the making of many books there is no end, and much study is a weariness to the flesh."

IV. 2 Timothy 4:13 speaks of a time when Paul asked Timothy to

_____.

V.   Remember: there are many good books out there that are helpful in study, but only one book is inspired by God (2 Timothy 3:16-17). All other books are written by men, and need to be read and used with caution (1 Corinthians 2:5).

Discussion

I.   Suggestions for a good library

    A. Concordances

1. *Cruden's Complete Concordance*

2. *Young's Analytical Concordance*

3. *Strong's Concordance*

B. Commentaries

1. *The Pulpit Commentary* (26 volumes)

2. *Truth Commentaries*

3. *Zerr Commentaries*

4. *Truth for Today Commentary*

5. *Barnes Notes*

6. *Keil and Delitzsch* (Old Testament Commentaries)

7. *Johnson's Notes* (New Testament Commentaries)

8. *Jamieson, Fausset and Brown Commentary on the Whole Bible*

9. *Adam Clarke's Commentaries*

10. *A Study of the Minor Prophets, Isaiah, Hailey's Comments* (Vol. 1 & 2), *Revelation* (all by Homer Hailey)

11. *Comments On Romans* by Bryan Vinson, Sr.

12. *Paul's Letter to the Saints at Rome* by R.L. Whiteside (Get at any cost!)

13. *Original Commentary on Acts* by J.W. McGarvey

14. *Acts Commentary* by Garreth Reese

15. *The Treasury of David* by Charles H. Spurgeon (also available as a download on e-Sword.net and other computer programs)

C. Bible dictionaries

1. *The New Unger's Bible Dictionary*

    2. *Zondervan Bible Dictionary*

    3. *Holman Bible Dictionary*

    4. *Vine's Expository Dictionary of New Testament Words* (Very good.)

D. Bible history books

    1. *The Complete Works of Josephus*

    2. *The Life and Times of Jesus the Messiah* by Alfred Edersheim

    3. *Eusebius*

E. Lexicons

    1. *Brown, Driver, and Briggs Lexicon*

    2. *Thayer's Greek-English Lexicon*

F. Bible reference books

    1. *The Interlinear Bible* by Jay P. Green, Sr.

    2. *The Treasury of Scripture Knowledge* by R.A. Torrey (Get this at any cost! E-sword.net supplies this free in its Bible program. It is also found in other places online.)

G. Sermon books

    1. *The Gospel Preacher (Vol. 1 & 2)* by Benjamin Franklin (Get at any cost!)

    2. *The Gospel Plan of Salvation* by T.W. Brents (Get at any cost!)

    3. *Gospel Sermons at the Mosque, God Hath Spoken,* and *Sermons on Church Trends* by Harris J. Dark (Get at any cost! Harris Dark was teaching at David Lipscomb during the heat of the institutional fight.)

4. *Franklin Road Sermons*

5. *The Arlington Meeting* (Get at any cost! This is a meeting of institutional and non-institutional brethren, talking about the heart of the issues!)

6. *Why I Left* (Get at any cost!)

7. *Gospel Meeting Sermons* by Johnie Edwards

8. *Sermons for the Seed Sower* by Johnie Edwards

9. *McGarvey's Sermons* by J.W. McGarvey

10. Sermon books outlining the New Testament by Curtis Flatt

11. *Hardeman Tabernacle Sermons* (5 volumes—volume 4 is out of print)

12. *Sermons Inside and Out* by Hoyt Houchen

H. Subject studies

1. *Is It Lawful?* edited by Dennis Allan and Gary Fisher

2. *A Review of "The Divorced and Remarried That Would Come To God"* by Weldon Warnock

3. *Life in the Son* by Robert Shank

4. *New Testament Christianity* by Z.T. Sweeney

5. *The Four-Fold Gospel* by J.W. McGarvey

6. *The Holy Spirit* by H. Leo Boles

7. *Muscle and a Shovel* by Michael Shank

8. Books by Robert Harkrider

9. Books by Bob Waldron

10. Books by Roy Cogdill

11. Restoration Reprint Library books published by College Press

12. *How to Study the Bible* by R.A. Torrey

13. *Instrumental Music* by Homer Hailey

14. *A Study of Premillenialism* by Tom O'Neal

I. Word studies

    1. *Wilson's Old Testament Word Studies*

    2. *New Testament Word Studies* by John Albert Bengel

    3. *Vincent's Word Studies of the New Testament* (4 volumes)

    4. *Word Pictures of the New Testament* by A.T. Robertson (Get at any cost!)

J. Biographies (Such books help put our lives in perspective and appreciate the sacrifices made in the past for us to preach today!)

    1. *J.D. Tant, Texas Preacher* by Fanning Yater Tant (sequel: *Nannie Yater Tant*)

    2. *What It Is, Is Preaching* by Robert F. Turner

    3. *The Search for the Ancient Order* by Earl Irvin West (There are 5 volumes, but volumes 4-5 reflect when West went with the institutional split.)

    4. *W.W. Otey, Contender for the Faith* by Cecil Willis (Considered the true volume 4 of West's series!)

    5. *Eye of the Storm* (a biography of the preacher Benjamin Franklin)

    9. *Memoirs of Alexander Campbell* by Robert Richardson

K. Debates (These works have brought many people out of error!)

    1. *The Neal-Wallace Discussion* (premillenialism)

2. Any Curtis Porter debate, you need to get and devour: *Porter-Waters Debate* (one cup and no Bible class), *Porter-Woods Debate* (institutionalism), *Porter-Bogard Debate* (baptism/general church question), *Porter-Myers Debate* (Is the church of Christ a denomination?), *Porter-Dugger Debate* (sabbath day or Lord's day?), *Porter-Tingley Debate* (Holy Spirit, baptism, faith only)

3. *Otey-Briney Debate* (instrumental music)

4. *Cogdill-Jackson Debate* (baptism/apostasy)

5. *Halbrook-Freeman Debate* (marriage-divorce-remarriage)

6. *Boswell-Hardeman Debate* (instrumental music)

7. *Cogdill-Woods Debate* (institutionalism)

8. *Woods-Nunnery Debate* (baptism/apostasy)

L. Books on preaching

1. *Preachers and Preaching* by James P. Needham (Get at any cost!)

2. *Preaching That Changes Lives* by Michael Fabarez

3. *Preaching with Freshness* by Bruce Mawhinney (A story that encourages you in preaching. Be careful—there are several denominational teachings mentioned.)

4. *The Seven Laws of Teaching* by John Milton Gregory

M. Out of print books (These are found at times when an older preacher wishes to sell some of his books, or when obtained at used bookstores or online. Keep your eyes open!)

1. *The Christ, the Cross, and the Church* by Larry Hafley (Get at any cost!)

2. Foy E. Wallace books are very good. Foy Wallace knew God's word and could communicate it in a very effective way! *Sermon on the Mount and the Civil State, Bulwarks of the Faith, The Gospel for Today, The One Book Analyzed and Outlined, The Instrumental Music Question, Number One Gospel Sermons*, and *God's Prophetic Word*. These are also available on CD.

3. *International Standard Bible Encyclopedia* by James Orr (Get his four volumes, not the "modernized" version of ISBE! This is available on e-Sword.net and on other Bible apps.)

4. *Preach the Word* edited by Earl Robertson

5. *Book, Chapter, and Verse* by Floyd Thompson

6. *Sermon Outlines on First Principles* by C.C. Crawford

7. *Reminiscences* by A.C. Grider

8. *They Heard Him Gladly* by Ottis L. Castleberry (a biography of the preacher Benjamin Franklin)

9. *Gospel X-Ray* by J.D. Tant

10. R.L. Whiteside books (*Reflections, The Kingdom of Promise and Prophecy, Doctrinal Discourses*)

11. *Preaching in a Changing World* by Irven Lee

N. Books recommended by others (I asked some preachers and elders what they would recommend a new preacher purchase for his library. Below are their suggestions of books not found above.)

1. A good English dictionary

2. Florida College lecture books

3. Truth Lectures books

4. Robert Harkrider's four volume set of workbooks called *Bible Basic Doctrines*

5. *Smith Bible Dictionary*

6. *Davis Bible Dictionary*

7. *From Creation to the Day of Eternity* by Homer Hailey

8. *The New Evidence that Demands a Verdict* by Josh McDowell

9. *A New Testament Commentary* by Wayne Jackson

10. *Reading Romans* by Robert Turner

11. *Letters to Young Preachers* edited by Warren Berkley and Mark Roberts

12. *The Holy Spirit* (workbook) by Heath Rogers

13. *The Gospel of Matthew* by Kenneth L. Chumbley

14. The *Truth for Today Commentary* series

II. Where can I find these books?

A. Used book stores: Different towns have different options here. Sometimes, a used book store can hold a treasure trove of books, including Goodwill.

B. Book stores: The books listed are written by brethren and are found at bookstores operated by our brethren. You don't generally find them in the mall at Lifeway or other Baptist bookstores!

C. The internet: There are some good references, Bible dictionaries and the like available for free on the internet. Some of the books mentioned above can be found there, as well as when they become public domain.

1. One website where public domain books are found is www.archive.org.

2. Logos is a Bible program that allows the purchase of reference books to help you in your study.

3. E-Sword is a free Bible program that allows the download of many free books, as well as the purchase of reference books (www.e-Sword.net).

Conclusion

I.   The list above is not intended to be exhaustive, but these are some of the major categories into which books fall, along with a list of many good writers that will help you in your Bible study.

II. Reminder: There are many good books out there that are helpful in study, but only **one** book is inspired by God (2 Timothy 3:16-17). All other books are written by men and need to be read and used with caution (1 Corinthians 2:5)!

~ 8 ~

Memorization

Introduction

I.   A preacher of the gospel needs to be filled and overflowing with the word of God if he is going to preach it and instruct folks in it.

II. The sooner this working knowledge of God's word is gained, the better you will be.

III. This knowledge helps self and others.

   A. David memorized Scripture, and it helped him in his life (Psalm 119:11). He said the blessed man meditates day and night on God's word. Certainly, memorization helps make this possible, because we can think of God's word while we are eating, sleeping, working, etc.

   B. Jesus knew and quoted Scripture when He was tempted (Matthew 4:1-11; Luke 4:1-13).

IV. In this study, work on your memorization of God's word.

Discussion

I.   Motivation for memorization

   A. What are some reasons for committing Bible passages to memory?

      1. It helps keep us from sin.

    a. Do you remember what David said in Psalm 119:11? He said he hid God's word in his heart for what purpose? _____

    _____

    b. As we noted above, Christ's correct handling of Scripture caused Satan to flee for a time (Matthew 4:1-11; Luke 4:1-13).

2. It instills a love for God's word.

    a. Just like feelings of love grow toward those we spend time with, so also we will have a greater love for God's word the more we spend time in it.

    b. Read Psalm 119:97 and take note of how often David meditated on God's word. _____

    c. On six other occasions in Psalm 119 (v. 48, 113, 127, 159, 165, 167), David specifically declares his love for God's word.

    d. These statements came as a result of his spending time in God's word, and "meditating" on it. The same will be true of us if we determine to spend time and meditate on God's word.

3. It causes us to meditate on the meaning of Bible passages.

    a. The concentration necessary for memory work demands that we meditate on the written word.

    b. As we think of the wording, phrases, the theme of our subject, the teaching being done in that context (all of which makes memory work easier), it helps us to meditate on the doctrine spoken by God (2 Timothy 3:16-17).

    c.   David called the one who would mediate in God's word a blessed man who delights in the word of God (Psalm 1:2). In light of Psalm 1:1-2, could God call me a "blessed" person?

4. It makes us familiar with the writers.

    a.   Isn't it frustrating at times to read a passage but not really be sure of the tone of voice someone used in a given situation? Sometimes, the tone of a voice can make all the difference in how something is said!

    b.   When we spend time memorizing passages, really concentrating on those words/phrases, the subject taught, the context of a passage, etc., to get its meaning, this allows us to know the writers better.

    c.   For example, after speaking of Diotrephes and how he acted, you can almost hear the urgency in John's words as he says, "Beloved, follow not that which is evil, but that which is good" (3 John 11). One can hear the frustration at times in Paul's tone when he writes to the Galatians, asking how they could be so soon removed from the grace of Christ to another gospel. Or when he said, "O foolish Galatians, who hath bewitched you, that ye should not obey the truth?" (Galatians 1:6, 3:1).

B. In our efforts to try to memorize passages, we learn the difference in the writings of Paul and John, as well as a difference in the writings of the other inspired writers of the Old and New Testaments.

1. This ought to cause us to marvel at how God could verbally inspire these men to write but at the same

time preserve their individual characteristics in their writings (2 Peter 1:20-21; 1 Peter 4:11; 1 Corinthians 14:37).

2. Memory work: what a blessing at our fingertips if we will work at it!

II. Some suggestions for memorizing Bible verses

A. Make flashcards with the verse on one side and the reference on the other side. Look at these daily.

B. Write out the verse(s) to memorize until you can write them perfectly. This involves not only the eyes and brain, but also the hands and sense of feeling.

C. Make a point to memorize the verses in your sermons, or at least the key verses in the sermon. Using the verses in a sermon or Bible class helps them to stick.

D. Brother Bill Cavender once told me it was easier for him to memorize sections/paragraphs of Scripture. He would go over a section slowly with thought and then begin trying to quote those sections. He was able to memorize a majority of the Bible in his life.

E. Be careful this doesn't turn into a cramming session. Rather, a constant meditation of God's word is key.

F. Folks like brothers James Needham and Franklin Puckett would memorize passages while they were plowing fields and doing other work as young men. A suggestion: try memorizing while mowing the yard or other similar kinds of work (hint: no distractions on a lawn mower!).

Conclusion

I. Keep up your memory work. Don't neglect this.

II.   Assignment #1: Do you know Psalm 23 by heart? If not, memorize this.

III. Assignment #2: Do you know 2 Timothy 4:1-5? Memorize this.

IV.   Assignment #3: Continue to challenge yourself daily/weekly to memorize more of God's word.

~ 9 ~
How to Study the Bible

Introduction

I.   There are many people who need to know how to go about a methodical study of God's word.

   A. Many Christians have no idea what it takes to "properly study" the Bible.

   B. Reading and studying are two different things!

      1. Read: "to peruse and apprehend the meaning of (something written, printed, etc.)" (*Webster's Encyclopedic Unabridged Dictionary of the English Language*)

      2. Study: "application of the mind to the acquisition (gaining possession) of knowledge, as by reading, investigation, or reflection" (ibid.)

         a. Please read Psalm 1:2 and 1 Timothy 4:15. The word "meditate" is used again. In the NAS, 1 Timothy 4:15 says, "take pains with these things; be absorbed in them."

         b. Reading is involved in studying, but when one reads, he is not necessarily studying!

         c. Some books to help you get started:
A Guide to Bible Study by J. W. McGarvey
How to Study the Bible by R. A. Torrey

Guide to Bible Study by James Tolle
Effective Bible Study by Howard Vos

C. Studying God's will is making that extra-concentrated effort to learn and know His will more perfectly. In study, take God's word and make it a part of you (example: Colossians 3:16a).

II. God expects His people to know His word (Deuteronomy 6:6-10; 2 Timothy 2:15; Ephesians 3:4).

III. For many, the question boils down to, "How do I study God's word?"

A. We might answer this question by suggesting verse-by-verse, a topical study, a book study, a character study, etc.

B. Please read Addendum 4 about: "Questions to Answer in a Book Study."

C. All of these things are fine and serve a purpose. Your choice often times is unique to you.

IV. In this study, observe some rules for studying the Bible. Regardless of whether a verse-by-verse study, a topical study, a book study, etc., is chosen, these rules apply.

Discussion

I. Observe who speaks.

A. Yes, this is an elementary point, but many fail here!

B. It is very important to know who is speaking in the material being studied. Why?

1. Because some are lying (Genesis 3:4, 4:8-9; Matthew 26:69-75).

2. Because some are teaching valuable lessons to be applied to self (Mark 16:16; Philippians 4:8; 1 Timothy 5:22; 1 Thessalonians 5:17; 1 John 5:2-3; Jude 3).

3. Because some speak from arrogance or a haughty mind (Daniel 4:30; Luke 18:10-14).

4. Because some speak from humility (1 Corinthians 15:9; Psalm 51:1-4).

C. By knowing who is speaking, we become better students of God's word.

1. This is because many people have their words recorded in the Bible.

2. Discerning between the words of Satan, the apostles, Christ, angels, publicans, Pharisees, etc., gives one a better understanding of the Bible.

II. Observe to whom God is speaking.

A. Not all laws commanded were intended for all men.

1. Examples:

a. Genesis 6:14: God didn't say this to you!

b. John 2:7: Is this command something we should do? (Remember rule #1).

c. Joshua 6:2-5: Are we to do this to please God?

2. Things commanded in the Bible cannot be dismissed. Note if the command is something to be obeyed.

a. Ephesians 6:1-4: Are these commands to be obeyed?

b. Romans 13:1-2: Is this command to be obeyed?

c. 1 Thessalonians 5:17-18, 21-22

d. 1 Corinthians 11:24-25

B. These observations are important so that correct conclusions are made.

III. Observe the context (setting).

A. This is key to determining whether or not the word of truth is being rightly divided.

    1. Example: "Man can fly." In context, that statement may very well be true.

        a. "There are lies in the Bible"—context! (Genesis 3:4, examples from part I, A, 1)

        b. Then again, this could be false if they are trying to say the Bible is not trustworthy.

    2. It is the same with the Bible. Statements cannot be pulled out here and there while thinking it leads to a knowledge of God's will.

    3. In talking to people, this is the one thing needing correction more than anything else!

B. Context—"the parts of a written or spoken statement that precede or follow a specific word or passage, usually influencing its meaning or effect" (ibid.) Remember A #1.

    1. In studying the context of a Bible passage, the verses before and after the one being studied need to be considered. The paragraph, chapter, or entire book may have to be read to grasp the context.

        a. Verse-by-verse or book study is ideal for figuring out the context.

        b. In topical study or character study, be careful that verses are not pulled out of their context in an effort to study.

    2. By knowing the context, false doctrine will be evident. Examples:

    a. Read Luke 5:20 then v. 17-25. Context makes a world of difference!

    b. Read Acts 8:35 (what "Scripture?") then v. 26-39. Isn't verse 35 easier to understand?

  3. Sometimes, just reading one or two extra verses throws a whole new light on the subject:

    a. Read John 6:44 then verse 45!

    b. Read Galatians 3:26 then verse 27!

    c. Read Romans 10:13 then verse 14-16!

C. If we ever wish to know God's word completely and apply it accurately, we need to understand the context of the passage.

IV. Observe the dispensation of the context.

A. Dispensation: "a divinely appointed order or age" (ibid.)

B. There are three dispensations (ages or periods of time) in the Bible: the Patriarchal, the Mosaic, and the Christian.

  1. Hebrews 1:1: God spoke in various means/ways to the people, including by prophets, but now speaks to us through His Son.

  2. Three ages are found in the Scripture: Patriarchal—2,500 years (Adam to Moses), Mosaic—1,500 years (Moses to John), and Christian (the cross to the end of time).

  3. Once the dispensation is known, the commands and examples will either be understood as applicable to us or as valuable lessons to gain knowledge (Romans 15:4).

C. This point confuses some. If there is not a proper division of the Bible, this gets us into trouble.

1. One man said, "If it is in there, I take it!" This is a dangerous attitude.

2. Examples:

    a. Noah built an ark (Genesis 6:14-17, 22). Since it is "in there" are we going to do that, too? No, it is a different dispensation (age) from us!

    b. "David used musical instruments, I think we could, too." Again: David lived in the Mosaic dispensation—under the Law of Moses. (Psalm 81:4; 2 Chronicles 29:25)

    c. Acts 2:42: This occurred in the Christian age.

D. Why do preachers use Old Testament passages from time to time? Why encourage study of the Old Testament?

1. Romans 15:4; 1 Corinthians 10:11: From the Old Testament, God's love, anger, plan for redemption, the creation of the world, patience, attitudes of people and how they have not changed much, etc., are seen.

2. God's prophecies in the Old Testament and their fulfillment in the New are seen.

    a. Isaiah 7:14 → Matthew 1:22-23

    b. Psalm 34:19-20; Zechariah 12:10 → John 19:36-37

    c. Isaiah 2:2-3; Daniel 2:44 → Acts 2

    d. This is a valuable part of the Bible!

3. God is consistent with men. Some laws and commands have not changed:

    a. Leviticus 19:18—Is this the only place? No! This is seen time and again throughout the Bible (Matthew 22:39; Romans 13:9; Galatians 5:14; James 2:8).

b. Hebrews refers continually to the days of Moses, showing that God's plan was working toward the end which we are a part of today. Romans also. One cannot understand the book of Revelation as he ought to without a knowledge of the Old Testament!

E. Therefore, respect the distinctions of the dispensations and apply them accordingly!

V. Use common sense.

A. We cannot jump into a verse or chapter and hope to know it all in a few minutes. It takes time and effort. Anything worthwhile takes time and effort (Ecclesiastes 12:12).

B. When studying the Bible, please notice:

1. Who the writer is/who is speaking (some are obvious, some are not)

2. What topics are addressed

3. Whether God is pleased or displeased with the people

4. Is this an Old Testament book, or a New Testament book?

5. The other rules studied

C. What we study and what we learn must be in harmony with all of the Bible. This shows good common sense.

1. A good way to study is to work on the easier things (milk) and consider the harder things (meat) in light of what we already know to be true.

2. If we see something from our study that makes the Bible sound contradictory, there is a problem with our study, and we need to go back and look at it again. The Bible does not contradict itself.

3. The Bible is its own best commentary—use it. You'll learn much on subjects you are studying if you'll find everything the Bible says on that subject and study it in that way! (Read the Old Testament in light of the New, etc.) This book is completely flawless. It has no contradictions and therefore will enlighten us in many ways (Psalm 119:105).

Conclusion

I. Now that we know these rules for Bible study, we can apply them to our study and make studying the Bible easier.

II. "I study my Bible like I plow my field"
A farmer explained, "I study my Bible like I plow my field. Often times when I'm plowing or breaking new ground, my plow will get hung under a root, and if I'm going at a pretty good clip it will really jar me. But I don't get mad and beat my mule and burn my plow. No, I just back up a little, ease over the root and get on with my plowing. Next time around I'll probably hit that root again and it still shakes me up, but I don't quit farming. I just back up, ease over the root and keep on working. Pretty soon I have hit that root so many times that it's loose, and the next thing you know I plow right through it and don't even notice it. I've got it shook loose.

That's the way I study the Bible. When I come upon a hard passage, it might shake me up a little bit, but I don't throw away my Bible and quit the Lord on that account. I just ease over it and keep on studying. The next time I read that passage I jar it a little bit more. I keep on doing this until finally, because of information that I have gathered from other parts of the Bible I am able to jar the passage loose. I understand it."—Author unknown

III. "Bible study is like going to my old well and getting a bucket of water. It's always water, but it's a bucketful you never had before!"—Laura Hall Sheridan Davis

~ 10 ~
Encouraging the Preacher to Write

Introduction

I. Just as oral communication is key when preaching the gospel, there is also a need for written communication when preaching the gospel.

II. There are some preachers who do not like to write, and this is unfortunate. Write articles to help both Christians and non-Christians.

    A. In this congregation, we take advantage of the printed page in bulletins, the newspaper, etc.

    B. There are several reasons for writing and developing this skill.

III. What good is the written word?

    A. It plants a seed in the minds of people.

        1. In fact, God's word is described as _____ (Luke 8:11; 1 Peter 1:23, 25).

        2. When this seed germinates in the heart, it produces fruit, "some a hundredfold, some sixty, some thirty" (Matthew 13:8).

        3. Perhaps a thought or two from this printed page can help in this work.

4. When one's heart is opened to the word, it can be won to the Lord (Acts 16:14).

B. It is a conversation starter.

1. Sometimes, folks want to talk to friends and neighbors about the gospel but don't know how to begin.

2. If you have written on various Bible topics, you might give them some of your writings to give to their friends and hopefully open a door to win someone to the Lord.

C. It stimulates further and deeper Bible study in people. You never know when a word, phrase or thought will spur someone to dig deeper and learn more about God's will.

Discussion

I. God places a premium on the printed page.

A. It is interesting to note that God considers the printed page of utmost importance in man's history.

B. God has His will recorded for us on the printed page (the Bible)!

1. Jesus asked the people, "Have you not read?" no less than seven times in the New Testament.

2. Some 82 times in the Bible, God's command to write something for the good of the people living at that time and for future generations is written.

C. Obviously, God thinks the printed page is important.

II. The advantages of the printed page

A. A part that is misunderstood can be reread as many times as necessary in order to understand it. In oral speech, one may or may not have such an opportunity to hear a misunderstood section again.

B. Another advantage is the ability of the reader to take the writing, lay it down for a while, and come back at a convenient time and continue in the reading when his mind is fresh.

C. The printed page lasts long after the writer is gone. It is through the printed page that one continues to teach others for years to come.

D. I hope that these thoughts will encourage you to write articles on Bible subjects, and to continue to improve in this work.

III. Some tips for good writing (bulletins, newspaper articles, etc.)

A. Use much Scripture. Your work as a preacher is the spreading of the gospel, so make sure that your writing is filled with it. Commentaries and the like are helpful in study, but do not allow the theories and commentaries of men to overtake your writings. Our job in writing, as in preaching, is to point people back to the Bible and what God says (1 Peter 4:11).

B. Write about the things you know. One cannot teach or write about things he does not know! Therefore, do not attempt to write on subjects, topics, or chapters which you have not studied (This same advice applies to Bible classes and sermons).

C. Consider the audience who is reading your writing. The subject matter chosen in a newspaper article will probably be different at times than the subjects chosen in a church bulletin.

1. Basic subjects are good for newspaper articles. Those reading the newspaper come from every walk of life, from atheists to your brethren in the congregation. Your purpose in a newspaper article is to grab the reader's attention and make them aware that the Bible is something they need to read.

2. Basic subjects are good for church bulletins, but church bulletins are also a medium where you get into the "meatier" subjects as well. The readership here (even if you mail them out) tends to be New Testament Christians who are interested in reading and studying God's word.

D. Use good grammar! "They ain't gonna take you serious without you writin good English and spellin words rite!"

1. For questions about grammar and correct spelling, consult a good dictionary. Also, go online and do a simple search to obtain answers to questions.

2. With few exceptions, the computer program being used will have an automatic spell checker. It will underline words that may be misspelled. Pay attention to the computer's suggestions.

3. Know when to capitalize words! Random capitalization is Distracting and It can Be Confusing to The Reader!

   a. Do you know when to capitalize words in a sentence? If not, look it up and write the rule here:

   _____

   _____

   _____

    b. Use ALL CAPS sparingly. At times, folks wish to emphasize words by capitalizing. However, in our social media mindset, all caps is considered shouting at someone.

    c. Emphasizing words is done by using **boldface**, or *italics*.

4. Some other pointers:

    a. When citing a passage of Scripture at the end of a sentence, abbreviate the book name, chapter, and verse inside parentheses. Example: (Mk. 16:16). Note: For help with this, please see Addendum 5 which gives the abbreviations for every book in the Bible.

    b. When citing a passage of Scripture within a sentence, write the book's complete name along with the chapter and verse. Example: In Colossians 3:16, we are taught to sing praises from the heart.

    c. When referring to deity in writing, capitalize the pronouns He, Him, His, etc. This may seem a little antiquated but is a good way to show respect for deity.

E. When writing for a newspaper, brotherhood magazine, church bulletin, etc., make sure to get the writing finished on time. Folks usually write on a deadline, so be respectful. Half the battle is won by showing up on time.

1. This is a reminder when dealing with people at the newspaper and the like. They are probably not Christians and know nothing of the church of Christ except what they see in people like you!

2. Do not leave them with the wrong impression. Do not take advantage of a situation.

3. Be on time. Hint: early is on time!

Conclusion

I. I hope that these rules are helpful to you as you continue to learn and grow as a writer.

II. Assignment #1: Write and prepare newspaper articles. Don't quit or give up. These articles not only serve you now but also in future times when you need to write articles in other places you live.

III. Assignment #2: Find your completed sermons and write articles on those same subjects.

A. Perhaps you will see that each point in your sermons could serve as an article at times.

B. Try your best to get your sermons pared down to one article apiece.

~ Addendum 1 ~
Do the Work of an Evangelist
Roger Shouse

"But you, be sober in all things, endure hardships, do the work of an evangelist, fulfill your ministry." (2 Timothy 4:5)

"Do the work of an evangelist." Those were the words of the aged, experienced and wise apostle Paul to the young preacher, Timothy. I've heard a lot about preachers recently. Some good, some not so good. I had lunch recently with a preacher that baptized me and was the catalyst into my becoming a preacher. Here we sat together at a table, and I found myself still asking him questions, still being mentored by him.

"Do the work of an evangelist." A simple statement. I gather that many churches and, from what I'm seeing, many preachers are not sure what that means. Let's look into this.

To start, consider what the work of the evangelist is not:

- **The preacher is not the guy who is available during the week to do what we can't.** I've sure seen that. Grandma needs to go to the doctor, and everyone is working—call the preacher. Now, why would folks do that? It is because they don't think he's doing much. Isn't he working too? Yard work needs to be done during the week—call the preacher. Someone needs a ride to the airport—call the preacher.

- **The preacher is not the handyman at the church house.** Ask the preacher to pick up trash after services, cut the lawn at the church building, fix a leaky facet in the bathroom at the church building…he's available, have him do it. Some even think that it's part of his job description.

- **The preacher is not the youth activity director.** Most preachers I know will do things with young people because they love people of all ages. But to think that it's the preachers job to have the kids in his home, arrange activities for the teens and keep the kids interested is not correct. Those are the things moms and dads ought to be doing. It's easy to pass them off to the preacher, and all the parents have to do is drop the kids off with a bottle of pop and leave the rest to the preacher. Sorry—not his job.

- **The preacher is not to solve all church problems.** Some problems are so complex and engrained in the fiber of the people that only the Lord can do something. A young preacher moves into a community to work with a church and within a few months he finds that the church is fussing and at odds with each other. He is told one side of the story and is expected to make things right. When he fails because people do not want to admit wrong and apologize or forgive, he is put into the hot seat and before long is asked to leave. Another young preacher is brought into that mess with the same expectations and the same results. Those folks ought to just shut the door and make up their minds if they want to follow Jesus or not. Some problems we must solve ourselves. Some problems are not the preacher's job to solve.

- **It is not the preacher's job to run the church.** He's not in charge of the place. He just happens to be the preacher. Some run to him as if he owns the church and pressure him to make decisions that are really not his to make. Because he has keys to the front doors does not mean that he runs the place. God ought to run the church. When we forget that, bad things usually happen.

Now, what is the preacher's job? It is to preach and teach God's word to everyone he can and to use every avenue he can to do that. This means the preacher will teach classes to many and to few. He will teach on Sunday morning and Tuesday afternoon. He will teach in the church building and in someone's front room. He will teach by email, letter, or phone call. He will preach in a church building or on video. He is to preach and teach God's word.

This necessitates that he understand God's word and know how to teach. It also necessitates that he understand how to connect with people and explain to them what God's word says. He is a teacher, but more—he is a preacher of God's word. His goal is not just informative but life-changing. He is trying to persuade people to follow Christ. He is using the teachings of Christ to change attitudes, behaviors and thoughts of people. His job is to preach and teach. That means warning when God has warnings. That means showing hope where God shows hope. That means instructing when God has instructions.

The greatest tool he uses is the Bible. He doesn't need strong arm tactics, cheap psychological tricks, or high-pressure gimmicks that force people into doing what they don't want to do. That is not his way. He wants people to want Jesus. He wants people to choose Jesus because they want Jesus and they see that they need Jesus.

The preacher may not be the smartest Bible student in a congregation. He may not even be the best public speaker among the congregation. He is the one who has decided to devote his life to pointing people to Heaven. His work involves helping those who have made messes of their lives. Poor choices, sinful habits and broken lives reveal the worst in us. A preacher with loose lips will not do well. A preacher who doesn't like people will not do well. A preacher with little patience will not do well.

His work necessitates studying. A person cannot teach what they do not know. He must read. He must like to read. He must think, consider, and get it himself. A man who doesn't like to read will struggle as a preacher. A man who can't think for himself will get in trouble as a preacher. He must do research. He must be able to explain clearly what the Bible says. He doesn't have to know everything that is false. He simply has to know what is right. The word "gospel" means "good news." His message, life and attitude ought to reflect that. His work surrounds the good news that the world needs.

One of Jesus' first parables was about a sower. He threw seed out in the fields. This is similar to the work of the preacher. Often, the preacher never sees the good that he has done. Often, it takes a long time for that seed to sprout, grow and become a mighty oak. The preacher doesn't worry about not seeing the results. He knows they will come. God is good. God gives the increase. His job is to get the word into the honest and good heart.

I have a son who is now preaching. I look at him and see myself more than 30 years ago. I have surrounded myself with some incredible preachers. They are some of my best friends in life. They have helped me so much. Preaching is a work. It's not for the lazy nor the guy who can't do anything else. It's not for the person who is not self-driven. I remember a preacher telling me years ago that after ten years, he ran out of ideas on what to preach about. He quit preaching. Is it any wonder?

Paul's words to young Timothy remain the best advice we could tell any preacher today: "Do the work of an evangelist." Get to it, preacher. There are those who need to know Jesus. There are those who need to be encouraged. There are those with doubts who need to be assured. Do the work. There's not enough time to golf every day. There's not enough time to play around every day. There's a work to be done. Do the work! Do it well!

~ Addendum 2 ~
Funeral Sermons

Preaching the Lost Into Heaven
Steve Wallace

Many of us have probably been to a funeral where an unsaved person was "preached into Heaven." By this we usually mean that, at the service for the deceased, a denominational "Pastor" or "Reverend" spoke of how the person had somehow come into a saved state shortly before death or spoke of them as if they were now in Heaven. There are several lessons that the living can learn from such events.

1. One must act on one's own behalf to get to Heaven. The preacher or teacher's work is to exhort others to save themselves or repent (Acts 2:40; 8:22). Christians should be good examples and shine as lights in the world (Phil. 2:15). However, the lost person also has something to do. If he has never come to Christ, he must hear the gospel, believe it, repent of his sins, confess Christ as the Son of God and be baptized for the remission of sins (Mark 16:15-16; Rom. 10:9-10; Acts 2:38). If an individual has once become a Christian and then later fallen away, such a one must repent and pray to God (Acts 8:22; 2 Cor. 7:10). If such people do not act in obedience to Christ's word it is meaningless to preach them into Heaven after they die. (It is equally meaningless to try to "fellowship" an erring brother into Heaven!) The lost and erring must come out of their sinful state.

2. "Care-giving" at the expense of preaching the gospel. In my opinion, one of the main reasons behind the practice of preaching the unsaved dead into Heaven is obvious: to comfort the grieving loved ones of the deceased. Such sermons are designed to show sympathy and care to those who remain behind. While God's people are told to weep with them that weep (Rom. 12:15), the practice under discussion is obviously an extreme we must avoid. Many a gospel preacher has used the opportunity of preaching someone's funeral to teach the truth to those who might otherwise not hear it. While not neglecting the comfort and consolation found in the word of God (2 Cor. 1:3-6), the preacher must balance his preaching to meet the spiritual needs of his listeners (2 Tim. 4:2). The main aim of a sermon should always be to bring people closer to the Lord. If we change the focus of our preaching to that of care-giving or making people feel good, we will have to come up with another message (Gal. 1:9), just like the denominational preachers do when they preach the lost into Heaven. It is this writer's conviction that the current trend of preaching lessons which lean heavily on human psychology or books on counseling for their support is a manifestation of this problem (2 Tim. 4:4).

3. Feigned love. The Christian is to love without dissimulation or falseness (Rom. 12:9; 2 Cor. 6:6). An obvious question arises with regards to the one who would claim to be a Christian and then try to preach a lost person into Heaven: Is this really showing love for lost souls? Who benefits from his message? Neither the living nor the dead. But he seems so loving as he stands there putting forth his message! Though most such preachers may be unaware of it, they are not showing true love to anyone in preaching the lost into Heaven. Using opportunities given us for speaking the truth in love will help us avoid such false displays of affection (Eph. 4:15).

Conclusion

Helping others get to Heaven involves instructing them in the ways of righteousness and encouraging them in that way (e.g., Acts 2:38-40). If we are truly concerned about the needs of our audiences, we will base our message to them on what the Bible says about their state and needs, encouraging them to apply God's word to their lives.

Guardian of Truth XL: 7 p. 19, April 4, 1996

Funerals and Gospel Preaching
Ron Halbrook (Midfield, Alabama)

The habits and customs associated with burying the dead vary from culture to culture and country to country. The range of differences includes superstitious rites and drunken feasts—everything on the spectrum from serious and pious to silly and pernicious. We live in a culture which permits, but does not dictate, funerals centered around devotion to God—prayers, sacred songs and Bible teaching. Christians and gospel preachers should not hesitate or be ashamed to use this wonderful opportunity for proclaiming the gospel of Christ in its purity and simplicity.

The use of such a format is not specified in Scripture but is authorized by every passage that mandates gospel preaching, beginning with Matthew 28:18-20 and on down the line. The habits of a culture and the setting of a society modify the format of opportunities for preaching Christ. But the context of the gospel is settled in Heaven and not subject to change. The facts, commands and promises of the gospel are the same for every culture and society—for all men!

> "For I delivered unto you first of all that which I also received, how that Christ died for our sins according to the scriptures; And that he was buried, and that he rose again the third day according to scriptures" (1 Cor. 15:3-4).

"And he said unto them, Go ye into all the world, and preach
the gospel to every creature. He that believeth and is baptized
shall be saved; but he that believeth not shall be damned"
(Mk. 16:15-16).

Opportunities which once existed in synagogues and public forums
for gospel preaching shifted in another time and place to open
fields, brush arbors and school houses, then to the town square,
and now to public media like newspapers, radio and television.
Formal debates as we know them involve unique features, such
as bringing false teachers into meeting houses built for preaching
the truth. No principle is violated; it is a format for accomplishing
the victory of truth and the harvest of souls. The Bible authorizes
gospel preaching—even debates with formal propositions,
moderators, bed-sheet charts, overhead transparencies and the
like—but does not specify those details. If the habits and customs
of a people open the door to gospel preaching on the occasion of
a wedding, a baby's birth or the solemn burial of the dead, we are
authorized to utilize that door.

Some brethren have scruples and would agree we can use the
funeral opportunity for gospel preaching only if we do so outside
of and away from the meeting house. "That is to be used only for
the Lord's work." Yes, and what is gospel preaching if it is not the
Lord's work? We can go to where the people are to do this work, as
Paul preached Christ in synagogues (Acts 9:20). Or, we can open
our meetings to those that are unbelievers so that they can come
to where we are (1 Cor. 14:23). And it does not change the case
whether we meet under a tree, in the personal dwelling place of a
member or in a meeting house built for the Lord's work.

If a people had the habit of calling upon God for guidance when a
new baby entered the family, we could go to a family or invite the
family into our meeting house in order to preach Christ to them.
This has nothing to do with infant baptism or infant membership

in the church and is used merely to illustrate. Where the family brought the baby in arms or not would not change the case, whether the couple to be married "dressed up" for the occasion or not would not change the case, whether the grieving people brought the casket with the dead in it (with or without flowers on the casket) would not change the case. From the vantage point of God's people, the point and the purpose is to preach the gospel of Christ, to reach the lost, to do the Lord's work!

To use such occasions and formats for preaching God's Word does not mean the church can build hospitals for babies to be born in, for engaged couples to obtain blood tests, or for dead people to be pronounced dead. The church is not authorized to build court rooms and to pay the salaries of civil judges to settle the legal ramifications of birth, marriage and death. There is no authority for, and this is no argument in favor of, the church conducting day care centers, newlywed showers or embalming services. We do have authority for local churches to use every possible format, arrangement and opportunity for gospel preaching.

Brethren, let's not hesitate to preach the gospel of Christ, both in arrangements by which people come to us and in arrangement by which we go to them. Funerals open wide the door to preach the great themes of the gospel—the certainly of death, the sinfulness of sin, judgment to come, the universal need of a Savior, the terms of pardon, the resurrection and the hope of Heaven through the forgiveness in Christ Jesus! What we preach, not the place where we preach it, is the vital thing.

David Lipscomb (1831-1917) was asked about funeral preaching and responded in the *Gospel Advocate* IX, 9 (28 Feb. 1867):173-74. In reprinting his article, we have italicized some of his words for emphasis. He beautifully painted the opportunities we may have in preaching Christ when death has come to someone's door. Let us be stirred to show genuine sympathy to our fellow man and to realize the highest degree of kindness we can bestow upon him is to teach him the truth and to direct him to the path appointed and marked out by God to lead mortals to Heaven.

Funeral Preaching
David Lipscomb

Brother Lipscomb: We hear very often in this country of our brethren preaching funerals. Now, when I joined the church it was the understanding that we were required to believe nothing but that which was taught plainly in the New Testament nor require anything else of others. I have searched diligently for command or example for it and have failed to find any. I may be blinded. Will some brother who preaches funerals tell us the chapter and verse, that we may no longer grope in darkness?

Yours in the one hope,
J.M. Mulliniks

Response: We certainly find no authority for preaching funerals in the Bible. But we do find authority to preach the Gospel, the word of life, in season and out of season, in other words, to be always ready to preach the word of life to dying men. The Christian must stand ever ready, watching and anxious, whenever occasion offers to point his dying fellow creatures to the Lamb of God who taketh away the sin of the world and to impress upon them a proper conception of the uncertainty and nothingness of life, the certainty of death, judgment to come and the awful weight and importance of eternity. This work can often be done effectually when death has come close to our own doors, snapt as under the tender tendrils of affection that entwine themselves around our own heart strings, and have taken from earth the dear idols of our hearts. In death— the death of a parent, brother, sister, child, or friend—God gives us a lesson on these subjects: the uncertainty of all things earthly, the certainty of death and of the necessity on the part of men to be prepared to pass the Jordan of death and enter the glorious home of the spirits of the just made perfect, rather than to be consigned to the dark abodes of death, to the eternal companionship of the Devil and his furies.

God in death teaches this lesson, but man in his mad career after the mammon of this world, in his vain search after happiness in the gratification of his appetites and passions, fails to read the lessons. Surely there is no harm, *can* be none, in the Christian man pointing him to this lesson and impressing it upon his heart while it is softened by sorrow and is opened, perhaps has been ruthlessly torn open, by the unrelenting hand of death. The Christian may then "in season" improve the lesson of God's teaching and pour into the torn and lacerated heart the healing oil of hope that is found in a confiding trust in Jesus, the anointed Savior. But when men preach something else besides the Gospel, when they teach that salvation can be gained otherwise than through a full and an entire acceptance of Christ in a submission to all of his appointments, evil is done. That this is frequently done in the discourses preached at the death of individuals is true. It is equally true that the same thing is done on divers other occasions. There is no more sin in making such an impression at the death of an individual than at other times. Such preaching is wrong, evil in its tendency and exceedingly sinful at funerals or any other times. The man that will cater to the prejudices and preach to please the friends of the deceased rather to please God, will preach to please man rather than God at other times and is unworthy to speak in the name of Christ.

The great need is men who love the truth better than they love popular favor, who had rather please God than man, who feel that the highest degree of kindness they can bestow upon their fellow man is to teach him the truth and to direct him to the path appointed and marked out by God to lead mortals to Heaven. Such men will preach the truth on all occasions in the love of it. Such a one that has confidence and trust in God and true Christian love for his fellow men can preach without evil influence or sin in the presence of the living and the dead, at a birth or a death, and he will always honor God and benefit his fellow man in preaching. But when a man preaches anything else than Christ and Him crucified, than justification through humbly following Christ in His appointments, walking in the ways He has marked out for us, that man does evil and is guilty of cruelly leading men down to endless death. Such preachers and such preaching should be discountenanced. Such preachers are unworthy to preach at funerals or away from them. Men of faith who love the truth, men of courage who can tell the truth, men of devotion who can suffer for the truth are the great crying needs of the church and the world.

Guardian of Truth XXVIII: 5, pp. 139-140, March 1, 1984

~ Addendum 3 ~
Acrostic Sermons

Speaking as the Oracles of God

Introduction

I.   The command to speak as the oracles of God is seen in both the Old and New Testaments.

    A.   Paul said that at one time the Jew was at an advantage over the Gentiles because they had the oracles of God (Romans 3:1-2).

    B.   The oracles of God are needful for God's people (both mature and babes in Christ—Hebrews 5:12-14).

II.   "We speak where the Bible speaks and are silent where the Bible is silent," was coined in the early 1800's and is still relevant today. Unfortunately, it is not practiced like it should be!

III. Text: 1 Peter 4:11

IV.   Look at this word "oracles" and see what it means to speak as the oracles of God.

Discussion

I.   Openly speak God's word

    A.   Do not be afraid to tell others about the gospel and about Christ.

1. John 18:19-21

2. He knew He had a specific mission in this life (John 18:37) and didn't have time to waste (John 9:4).

B. Be a people who openly invites people to hear God's word and openly invites them to study.

1. The truth does not fear investigation.

2. Be open with people, let them ask us questions, and let us ask them questions!

3. This includes our children and family members.

  a. Deuteronomy 6:6-9

  b. Ephesians 6:4

  c. Matthew 10:37: We must not "love" our family so much that we refuse to tell them the truth.

II. Ready

A. 1 Peter 3:15 (to answer, Colossians 4:6)

B. Romans 1:15 (ties into point #1)

C. 2 Timothy 4:6 (to be offered)

D. If the Bible stresses nothing else, it stresses the importance of preparation!

III. Attitude

A. I must have the right attitude toward others if I am to "S.A.T.O.O.G!"

1. I must have the attitude of Philip, willing to teach God's truth (Acts 8:30).

2. I must have the eunuch's attitude, willing to listen when others speak (Acts 8:31).

B. Proper attitude stressed:

   1. Proverbs 23:7a

   2. Matthew 15:18-20

C. These things are necessary in all walks of life! I must have the proper attitude toward:

   1. Fellow Christians (Ephesians 4:31-32)

   2. Co-workers (Matthew 7:12)

   3. Spouse (Ephesians 5:23-33)

   4. The opposite sex (Matthew 5:27-28)

   5. The church (Matthew 16:18; Colossians 1:18; Romans 12:5)

   6. Satan (John 8:44; 1 Peter 5:8)

IV. Christ

A. Christ MUST be my focus in all things, and especially as I "S.A.T.O.O.G." (Colossians 3:17).

B. How am I doing along this line? Is my focus on Christ or on self?

C. When Jesus was upon this earth, He didn't please Himself (John 12:49-50; Hebrews 10:9). Why do I think I am entitled to do this?

D. Most, if not all, of the evil that occurs in society today would be gone if we focused our lives on Christ, looking forward to Heaven when we die (Philippians 3:13-14)!

E. Let us make sure we are focused on Christ!

V. Learn

A. To "S.A.T.O.O.G" we must learn what the book of God says.

    1. Philippians 4:8-9

    2. How is this done? (Miraculously?)

       a. Ephesians 3:4

       b. 2 Timothy 2:15

  B. Remember: I cannot speak what I do not know!

VI. Example

  A. I am a walking, talking example. Let me make sure I am setting the right one.

    1. Matthew 5:14-16

    2. 1 Timothy 4:12

    3. 2 Corinthians 3:2

  B. S.A.T.O.O.G. means I will be an example to those who aren't. It means I am setting an example before the next generation of how they are to act.

  C. What kind of an example are you leaving? The kind that says God's word is only important when I have time?

VII. Salvation (eternal)

  A. This must be what we are striving for every day.

    1. Now you can see why it is so important to:

       a. Have the right attitude

       b. Set the right example

       c. Speak where the Bible speaks and be silent where the Bible is silent before it is too late

Conclusion

I. Come now and be saved!

Watch

Introduction

I. "Watch" is a word used often in describing a Christian's life.

    A. Paul told the Ephesians (Acts 20:31)

    B. The Corinthians: (1 Corinthians 16:13-14)

    C. The Colossians (Colossians 4:2)

    D. The Thessalonians (1 Thessalonians 5:6)

    E. Timothy (1 Timothy 4:5)

    F. Jesus to church at Sardis (Revelation 3:2-3)

II. In thinking about this subject, I want to present an acrostic lesson on the word watch. From each letter I want to suggest some lessons we can take with us.

Discussion

I. <u>W</u>

    A. Worship

        1. It must be "in spirit and in truth" (John 4:24).

            a. In connection with spiritual matters and with the truth

            b. God demanded it in Joshua's day (Joshua 24:14) and demands it today.

        2. Our worship must contain:

            a. The right motive (John 4:24)

            b. The right acts: singing, praying, teaching, giving, taking the Lord's Supper (Acts 2:42, 20:7; Eph. 5:19; 1 Cor. 16:1-2)

            c. The right day: first day of the week (Acts 2:42, 20:7)

3. This is not party time or a time to get free babysitting. This is not a fashion show or time to catch up on gossip. We meet for the purpose of worshipping God and must do so in a reverent manner.

4. A lot of churches do not do this, but we must stand and follow what is right.

B. Walk (course or manner of life)

1. I am to walk the strait and narrow way (Matthew 7:13-14).

2. Walk after the spirit (Romans 8:1), focused on spiritual matters (Romans 8:5-6).

3. Walk honestly (decently, Romans 13:13-14).

4. Walk by faith (2 Corinthians 5:7).

5. Refusal to do this results in my walking toward destruction and eternal damnation. It is important that I watch where I am walking spiritually.

C. Work

1. What are you doing? Are the things you're doing well-pleasing to God?

2. I need to make sure I am working the works of God (John 9:4; 1 Peter 2:21-22).

3. Remember Ephesians 2:10 as well as Hebrews 13:20-21.

II. <u>A</u>

A. Aim

1. What is my focus or goal in life? Is it a new car? Great job? Big house, etc.?

2. The Christian's aim or focus is Heaven (Matthew 6:19-21; Colossians 3:1-2).

3. If I allow smaller things to draw me away from my goal, I may not make it. I need to make sure that I am not short-sighted in my journey.

B. Actions

1. Every move I make in life needs to be leading me to the Master. If it's not doing that, then I am going the wrong way; I am not acting right.

2. Read what Jesus said in Matthew 12:30. There is your choice: will you be with Christ or against Him? Our actions bear this out, for they truly speak louder than our words do.

3. Go back to point A: my aim determines my actions, for what my mind decides is what I do.

C. Army

1. The picture of a solider is seen several times in the New Testament. A Christian is a soldier in the Lord's army.

2. As such, the Lord is our captain (Hebrews 2:10), we are subordinate to Him (2 Timothy 2:3-4) and we wear the armor necessary for battle (Ephesians 6:11-17).

3. We are to "war a good warfare" (1 Timothy 1:18). This war is against Satan (2 Cor. 10:4-6).

III. T

A. Time (It is slipping away!)

1. God teaches us to redeem the time (Ephesians 5:16). David asked God to teach us to number our days (Psalm 90:12).

2. Take advantage of the time we have on this earth (John 9:4). Look at what Christ did (John 21:25).

How was this possible in just three years? Because Christ took advantage of His time and His opportunities to teach and to pray.

B. Talent

   1. God has given us all some type of talent that we need to develop. See the songs "Oh The Things We May Do" and "Room In God's Kingdom" (*Sacred Selections*, #79 and #80).

   2. Matthew 25:14-30: Remember that the one punished was the one who squandered his talent. He did not develop or use what he had, and he suffered for it.

C. Tongue

   1. This is dangerous, for it is an "unruly evil." Read: James 3:2-12

   2. Based on what James has said, we know it is dangerous if we do not watch our tongues. (Further warnings: Ephesians 4:25, 29, 31; Colossians 3:9).

IV. <u>C</u>

A. Company

   1. 1 Corinthians 15:33; 2 Corinthians 6:14-17: The company we keep has an effect on us.

   2. Jesus' close associates were: (1) God and (2) the Apostles.

B. Character

   1. "My reputation is what the world thinks I am; my character is what God thinks I am" (Tant).

   2. Do I have the character of Abraham? Moses? Daniel? Sarah? Jochebed? Mary? If not, why not? Let's do what we can to follow in the footsteps of these godly men and women.

C. Church

    1. The church, Christ's body, must be pure. Therefore, we are responsible for:

        a. Demanding that the truth be taught (1 Thessalonians 1:8)

        b. Keeping self pure (1 Timothy 5:22; Philippians 4:8-9)

        c. Knowing God's will (Ephesians 3:4; 2 Timothy 2:15)

        d. Not allowing false teachers or false concepts to get a foothold (Galatians 1:6-9)

V. <u>H</u>

A. Heart

    1. Proverbs 4:23; Matthew 12:34b-35, 15:18-19

    2. Acts 4:13: What do people say about you?

B. Hands ("Oh, be careful little hands what you do")

    1. Ecclesiastes 9:10: In our physical life, we are commanded to provide for our families (Ephesians 4:25; 1 Timothy 5:8).

    2. Just as well, we need to remember that our hands need to be about the Lord's work. We need to work just as hard or harder for the spiritual as we do for the physical. Many get this reversed.

        a. Matthew 6:33

        b. 1 Timothy 6:11-12

    3. This must be done "from the soul."

C. Home

1. Many songs have been sung about home. We think of our parents' home and sweet memories of childhood.

2. Understand though, there is a home far better than that: our home promised and prepared in Heaven (John 14:1-3).

3. We need to make sure and keep our eyes on the goal. Let us watch and be ready for Heaven. Let us be prepared so that whether we die or the Lord comes for us that we are ready to enter into the land of cloudless day and the joys of an eternal day with God.

Conclusion

I. Are you watching? Have you started yet?

II. Come now.

~ Addendum 4 ~
Questions to Answer in a Book Study

(Source: Torrey, R.A., *How To Study The Bible*, p. 17-18)

1. Who wrote the book?

2. To whom did he write?

3. Where did he write it?

4. When did he write it?

5. What was the occasion of his writing?

6. What was the purpose for which he wrote?

7. What were the circumstances of the author when he wrote?

8. What were the circumstances of those to whom he wrote?

9. What glimpses does the book give into the life and character of the author?

10. What are the leading ideas of the book?

11. What is the central truth of the book?

12. What are the characteristics of the book?

~ Addendum 5 ~
Books of the Bible and Their Abbreviations

Genesis = Gen.

Exodus = Ex.

Leviticus = Lev.

Numbers = Num.

Deuteronomy = Deut.

Joshua = Josh.

Judges = Judg.

Ruth = Ruth

1 Samuel = 1 Sam.

2 Samuel = 2 Sam.

1 Kings = 1 Kngs.

2 Kings = 2 Kngs.

1 Chronicles = 1 Chron.

2 Chronicles = 2 Chron.

Ezra = Ezra

Nehemiah = Neh.

Esther = Est.

Job = Job

Psalms = Ps.

Proverbs = Prov.

Ecclesiastes = Ecc.

Song of Solomon = Song Of Sol.

Isaiah = Isa.

Jeremiah = Jer.

Lamentations = Lam.

Ezekiel = Ezek.

Daniel = Dan.

Hosea = Hos.

Joel = Joel

Amos = Amos

Obadiah = Obad.

Jonah = Jon.

Micah = Mic.

Nahum = Nah.

Habakkuk = Hab.

Zephaniah = Zeph.

Haggai = Hag.

Zechariah = Zech.

Malachi = Mal.

Matthew = Matt.

Mark = Mk.

Luke = Lk.

John = Jn.

Acts = Acts

Romans = Rom.

1 Corinthians = 1 Cor.

2 Corinthians = 2 Cor.

Galatians = Gal.

Ephesians = Eph.

Philippians = Phil.

Colossians = Col.

1 Thessalonians = 1 Thess.

2 Thessalonians = 2 Thess.

1 Timothy = 1 Tim.

2 Timothy = 2 Tim.

Titus = Titus

Philemon = Phile

Hebrews = Heb.

James = Jas.

2 Peter = 2 Pet.

2 Peter = 2 Pet.

1 John = 1 Jn.

2 John = 2 Jn.

3 John = 3 Jn.

Jude = Jude

Revelation = Rev.

www.ingramcontent.com/pod-product-compliance
Lightning Source LLC
Chambersburg PA
CBHW060035050426

42448CB00012B/3016